London Transport
in the 1950s

Michael H. C. Baker

Contents

First published 2000

ISBN 0 7110 2688 2

Published by Ian Allan Publishing

an imprint of Ian Allan Publishing Ltd, Terminal House, Shepperton, Surrey TW17 8AS; and printed by Ian Allan Printing Ltd, Riverdene Business Park, Hersham, Surrey KT12 4RG.

Code: 0009/B1

Introduction

There can be few decades in the history of road transport in the capital which saw more changes than the 1950s. The decade began with the elimination of the tram from the streets of London; by the middle, production of the RT family — the most numerous type of bus ever designed for service with one operator in the UK — was complete; next came the prototype of its successor (the Routemaster, many hundreds of which are still at work in London); whilst by the end of the period the trolleybus was on its way out.

London is no ordinary city. It is the capital of what was once, for better or worse, the greatest empire the world has seen. In 1945 not everyone believed those days were over. Pageantry was (and is) part of everyday life in London. Many of the visitors from Australia, Canada, South Africa and elsewhere in the late 1940s still regarded London as home; Americans came to renew wartime memories; whilst from the Caribbean and the Indian sub-continent Commonwealth citizens were encouraged to emigrate and work for London Transport. The red double-deck bus has come to be such a symbol of London that members of the RT class and its successor the Routemaster — as well as various red-painted Bristol FLF and VR impostors — can be found in tourist spots all over the world. From Niagara Falls to Sydney Harbour, these vehicles provide nostalgic reminders of their original home city.

At home London Transport has always been a key player in the great dramatic or ceremonial public events, usually in the off-stage role of provider of transport but sometimes taking the limelight itself. Huge numbers of buses, trams, trolleybuses and coaches helped evacuate London children to the main line stations and to the country at the outbreak of war in 1939. Our family moved to Bournemouth in 1944 after the windows and most of the roof of our house were blown away by a nearby doodlebug explosion. A year later, I knew for sure that the war was really over when, at the end of our train journey back from the Hampshire coast, we boarded a route 18 'Feltham' tram outside Waterloo station to take us home to Thornton Heath Pond.

Another year on and my father and I watched RT4 and RT39 take part in the Victory parade. Later there would be the 1948 Olympic Games, the 1951 Festival of Britain and the Coronation of 1953. For all of these occasions London Transport curtailed its regular services as necessary and laid on special ones, for competitors, participants and for the general public. All these events entailed

The electric tram had begun work in London in 1901 and the largest class of all — the LCC's 'E/1' type, 1,000 of them — dated originally from 1906. Many lasted until the early 1950s, antiquated and totally unfashionable, but still perfectly roadworthy.
No 1813, one of the later ones built in 1922, is seen in Kennington looking pretty spruce and ready for a good many more years' service, although in fact it had only months to go.
All uncredited photographs are from the author's collection

3

much preparation and for the Coronation in particular London really went to town in decorating the streets along which the Queen would process. London Transport kept a fleet of buses in reserve, a number of them elderly but tidied up STLs, to operate Festival of Britain and Coronation route tours.

Then there were annual events, such as the Derby and the Lord Mayor's Show. Sometimes the latest London buses — RM1, for instance — would take part in the latter. Whilst, at the opposite end of the time-scale, petrol-engined veterans — STs, LTs and Tilling STLs with sagging bodies living on borrowed time — would growl and gasp their way up the leafy Surrey slopes amongst the hired open-toppers and coaches to Epsom Downs.

All this was long ago and generally the part played today by London Transport in such great events is more peripheral. Yet out of the Coronation Route Tours grew the huge number of sightseeing tours seen in central London today, provided by a bewildering number of double-deck buses in many liveries, usually open-topped, ranging from former Southdown 'Queen Mary' Leyland PD3s through to Routemasters and imported six-wheelers.

The less glamorous end of the market, but of great economic consequence, is suburbia. Growing up in a quiet road of houses built upon what had been farmland until the last years of the 19th

5

century one envied those who lived in really interesting places which featured in history books. It got embarrassing explaining to strangers where Thornton Heath was. It wasn't until I had moved away and could look back with greater objectivity that I realised Thornton Heath, like everywhere else, had a history. You have to dig rather deeper, listen more carefully, pay attention to nuances and patiently ferret out from parish records, local newspapers and ancients' memories the stories every suburb has to tell.

Bus, train and tram timetables help tell these stories, just as do postcards, which so often feature public transport and a few of which we have reproduced. In the 1940s and for much of the 1950s, nearly everyone in suburbia relied upon public transport. This enabled the population to get to work, which usually meant heading towards the City or the West End, to school, which often involved cutting across the primarily north-south traffic flow, or out into the country at weekends. We have focused chiefly on trams, trolleybuses and red motorbuses but there was yet another dimension to the London Transport story — the Country Area.

Strangers naturally enough assumed that the fleet of green-painted double- and single-deck buses — proportionally a lot more of the latter compared to the Central Area — spent its days amongst pleasant country lanes and market towns. Some parts did but an awful lot of it was more familiar with suburbia. Ribbon development, until restricted in the late 1930s, drove fingers of suburbia deep into rural Kent, Surrey, Buckinghamshire (the Metropolitan Railway had already done for Middlesex), Hertfordshire and Essex. This brought much business for Country Area and Green Line routes and is as much a part of the period covered in this book as trams and trolleybuses.

The 1950s were not propitious for the future of electrically powered street transport in Britain; unless you were a milk float. Nearly all the remaining tram systems disappeared and the trolleybus ones were following. Streets were becoming more congested and the tram, which passengers often had to board by

walking out from the pavement, and the trolleybus with its fixed route and reduced speed through junctions, were seen as the chief villains. Now, of course, we know they were the chief victims and the modern articulated tram, with its tremendous capacity, has made a remarkable comeback, none more dramatic than in my home town of Croydon. Here, someone with a delightful sense of the appropriateness of things has decreed that the number of the first new tram should immediately follow on from the highest-numbered car in the original London fleet, ex-LUT 'W' type No 2529.

At the start of a new century, it is a frightening and sobering thought that almost all the scenes illustrated here are now almost 50 years old. Several are of a later period but show scenes that were commonplace in the 1950s. Most of the vehicles portrayed are as much a part of history as the earlier types that they were designed to replace. The one exception to this is the Routemaster; if anything epitomises continuity and change in the Metropolis it is this product of the 1950s. As the 50th anniversary of the prototype approaches, the skills of the designers and builders of the RM can still be seen daily in central London.

Michael H. C. Baker
Dorset, Summer 2000

The LPTB

The London Passenger Transport Board came into existence in 1933, replacing the various municipal and company operators, including London County Council. By 1939, notwithstanding the slow climb out of recession, it had gained for itself a pre-eminent place amongst passenger transport systems as a result of the energy and vision displayed under the chairmanship of Lord Ashfield and Frank Pick as Managing Director. A highly standardised fleet of trolleybuses had swept away more than half the vast tram fleet, much of it obsolete, inherited from its predecessors. Its latest diesel-engined double- and single-deck buses and Green Line coaches provided the highest standards of comfort and reliability. Pick's friend, the architect Charles Holden, had given London Transport some wonderful-looking stations to complement its headquarters, 55 Broadway. The latter, completed in 1930, was graced by two stone figures carved by the great sculptor, Jacob Epstein. Elsewhere, many gifted artists had been commissioned to provide posters that brightened the capital and suburbs.

Design was given the highest possible priority and consequently just about everything introduced since 1933 — buses, trolleybuses, coaches, Underground trains, buildings, posters, maps, timetables etc — looked good. Then came the war.

London suffered greatly, although it is remarkable that in the area which suffered worst of all — the East End around the docks — the trams, trolleybuses and motorbuses serving it escaped relatively unscathed. Throughout the duration of the war 15 LT trolleybuses, 77 trams and 166 buses and coaches were destroyed by enemy action, whilst there were 7,046 incidents involving damage. On top of this the vehicles which emerged unscathed had received nothing like the maintenance which they had come to expect in peacetime. Many were overdue for replacement anyhow, including the entire tram fleet, the replacement programme having ground to a halt in 1940, although the last trolleybus built to peacetime standards was not completed until the following year.

There were still many buses of pre-LT origin to be seen at work over the entire network. These would have been withdrawn, had not the war intervened, whilst the majority of the standard STLs were also looking pretty tired and needed urgent tender loving patching up to keep them running into the 1950s. The single-deck classes and the trolleybuses had fared rather better and, curious though it might seem, so in a sense had the trams for they were tough old

veterans, with plenty of elderly but still quite serviceable 'E/1s' withdrawn but kept in reserve should they be needed. Some 'E/1s' dating back to Edwardian days lasted until late 1951, although the few which were still in service on the last day, 5 July 1952, were of 1930 origin — which seemed ancient enough then, yet today there are 40-year-old Routemasters still at work in London.

Sifting through the hundreds of pictures whilst making my selection for this book, one of the most abiding impressions is how shabby many parts of London were, especially the inner suburbs, throughout the period. A German friend of mine, who had been a small child in the Ruhr during the war and who had settled here in 1961, reminded me recently of this. 'By then,' she said, 'much of Germany had been completely rebuilt but parts of London looked as if the war had only just ended'. Indeed the neglect went back further, to the depressed days of the 1930s. One has only to look at the background, to the people as well as their surroundings, in so many bus, tram and trolleybus pictures in Deptford, Brixton, Kentish Town and elsewhere, to see the truth of this. Not that the world has turned around completely, even by the late 1990s. I recently had a ride in the preserved 1934-vintage STL469 from Ash Grove garage to Covent Garden, and the journey along Bethnal

◄ London Transport is justly respected as a pioneer of bus preservation. In this July 1946 picture D189, a CWA6 Daimler with early postwar Park Royal bodywork newly delivered to Sutton Garage, passes 'Ole Bill', one of the London General B-type which carried troops to the trenches during World War 1, being prepared for a rally in Regent's Park. *Fox Photos/ Ian Allan Library*

Another 1946 delivery was this all-Leyland PD1, STD133, standing at the Greenford terminus of the 55, ahead of an ST and a B, the latter being a wartime Bristol delivered in 1942.

A well-known terminus for a number of East London bus routes was the Royal Forest Hotel on the edge of Epping Forest. The postwar RT makes its first appearance in this book, fourth from left. First left is a wartime G class Guy, then an STL, another G, whilst to the right of the RT are two STs.

Green Road, past shuttered shops and derelict, once elegant grey/yellow early 19th century brick tenements, could only be likened to a trip back through time.

The arrival of thousands of immaculate, superbly finished members of the RT family from 1947 onwards transformed the look of many London thoroughfares. All of this presented a fascinatingly kaleidoscopic scene to a young spotter such as myself. The least favoured were the wartime Guys and Daimlers — I don't think I ever saw one of the small number of Bristols — for they looked and were primitive, both inside and out, well below the usual London standards. This did not mean they were uninteresting. On arriving at Victoria on one of our expeditions to the West End I would sometimes badger my mother into boarding a Guy on the 76 to take us to Westminster just to experience its basic interior.

Two of our local garages, Merton and Sutton, stocked up on Daimlers; indeed, apart from the Green Line ones, they had the lot and even the green ones came to Merton eventually. I wonder who thought such basic vehicles, even if brand-new, were suitable Green Line material? Some of the wartime buses were so primitive they even had wooden seats. Not surprisingly, few were allowed into the City or the West End. Just five routes, Guys on the 23 and 76 and Daimlers on the 77, 77A and 88, had a regular allocation, plus the 11 STDs of 1941-2 that worked out of Gillingham Street behind Victoria station.

In 1948 the LPTB was nationalised, along with the 'Big Four' railway companies (and a number of other lines), as part of the British Transport Commission and was retitled the London Transport Executive. This transfer, as will be seen during the course of the book, was to have a dramatic impact upon the plans of the LPTB, particularly for expansion of the Underground network. In view of the need for massive investment in the main line railways and by the costs of postwar reconstruction, many of the schemes envisaged by the LPTB came to nothing. Throughout the decade recorded in this book, the LTE had direct control of London's transport, both road and rail; it was not until 1963, with the abolition of the British Transport Commission, that London Transport became an independent board answerable directly to the Ministry of Transport.

The first non-roofbox RTs appeared in the autumn of 1948. Brand-new RT1125 swings elegantly above an inspection pit at Aldenham Works shortly before entering service in February 1949 from Muswell Hill garage.
London Transport Museum

Although single-deck vehicles have formed an increasingly significant proportion of the fleet since the 1980s, they had always worked many outer suburban routes and here TD67, a Mann Egerton-bodied Leyland PS1 Tiger delivered in February 1949 to Harrow Weald garage for the 221 from North Harrow to Pinner (a 22min journey) stands at the Pinner terminus two months after entering service. Alongside is a prewar all-Leyland TD4, STD97 of Hendon garage, which is running on the 183.

9

There were occasions when single-deck buses appeared on central London routes, but it took something special for this to happen. One such time was an acute vehicle shortage in 1948. STs, LTs and STLs were taken off the road in large numbers, having been declared unfit for service. The delivery of new buses of the RT family could not keep pace with these depredations and so an assortment of buses and coaches was hired. One of the more eye-catching was this splendid beast, a six-wheel Albion from Scotland. It is seen in the Strand in the company of pre- and postwar STDs, an STL and an LT.

The AEC Regal T class was introduced in 1929, but there had been many variations since then, the last variant arriving in 1948. Some of the early ones were remarkably long-lived. Eighteen, including T32 seen here, were refurbished by Marshalls of Cambridge and fitted with oil engines taken from scrapped STLs, continuing to work from Kingston garage on the 218 and 264 routes until 1953. *F. G. Reynolds*

London also borrowed — did it ask first? — a number of brand-new ECW-bodied Bristol double-deck vehicles. Most were lowbridge buses, which convinced Londoners to keep well clear of Tilling territory whenever possible, but there were some highbridge examples. One such was Brighton, Hove & District K5G No 6404, which went to Tottenham garage to work the 73. The bus is seen here at Richmond bus station in late 1949 pictured in full Brighton livery but without fleetname.

Trams

In many ways, London's trams were an anachronism at the start of the 1950s. If war had not intervened, they would have been consigned to the history books well before the era covered by this book. In the event, however, World War 2 and postwar shortages ensured that the trams were destined to live longer, albeit increasingly run down. With some 800 trams in service in the mid-1940s, London could still claim to have the second biggest tramcar fleet in the British Isles, but this was soon to change. A revitalised policy of conversion — Operation Tramaway — was announced in July 1950 and, over the next two years, the surviving routes and vehicles were to succumb to the motorbus.

The London tram fleet comprised vehicles acquired from a number of sources: the former London County Council, the former municipalities and three companies — the Metropolitan Electric Tramways, the London United Tramways, and the South Metropolitan Electric & Lighting Co — that collectively had served London prior to the creation of the LPTB in 1933. The ex-LCC 'E/1s', of which 1,000 had been built, were Edwardian in origin. This meant they belonged to the era of the normal control, solid-tyred, open-top B type petrol-engined bus, a museum piece of such antiquity I assumed it to be roughly contemporary with Stephenson's *Rocket* and the Pyramids. Nowadays, a touch of wood in a car interior is considered very up-market, but the 'E/1' contained little else and there was nothing up-market about an 'E/1'. The trams upon which I regularly travelled — the ex-Croydon and Walthamstow corporations versions of the 'E/1', the 'E/3s' and the 'Felthams' — were all rather superior. The 'Feltham' was, of course, the finest thing to run on rails, with the possible exception of a GWR dining car.

London tram tracks were unique in that a perfect indication that the outer suburbs were being left behind and the heart of the capital was approaching was the change from overhead to conduit. The LCC had insisted on the conduit system to avoid what it considered unsightly overhead, although this never seemed to be an issue elsewhere. Be that as it may, Embankment-bound trams from Croydon switched from overhead to conduit collection at the bottom of the hill by Streatham station, leading up to St Leonard's church. I could never understand why this — the station, not the church — didn't exchange names with a station that was called Streatham Hill which was a mile or so to the north, not far from

A majestic 'Feltham', No 2141, heads through Kennington on the peak hour route 22 from Savoy Street, Embankment, to Tooting. In the distance are a couple of RTs, with an 'E/1' tram peering out from behind the leading one.

11

Telford Avenue Depot, with not a hill in sight. But then Streatham Common station was a long way from Streatham Common, so perhaps it was all due to a perverse naming policy of the London, Brighton & South Coast Railway.

Telford Avenue was chosen as the new home of the 'Felthams' when they moved south in the late 1930s. This was partly because the depot, with very little structural alteration, could accommodate them and partly because of the trams' potential speed on the long and straight stretches of the Brighton Road south of Norbury. Not only was a 'Feltham' fast, but its weight ensured that it could coast with power off for considerable distances.

With the replacement of the trams and the migration of the 'Felthams' to Leeds, Telford Avenue depot was replaced by the present bus garage on the same site but renamed Brixton, adding yet more confusion to the naming of transport facilities in that part of south London. Likewise, down at the bottom of the hill the impressive municipal building in the heart of Brixton was — and is — called Lambeth Town Hall.

Next door to Telford Avenue was Brixton Hill depot, which also housed 'Felthams'. Perhaps surprisingly it still stands with 'LCC Tramways, 1924' emblazoned over its doorway, and, most remarkably, a section of track is visible, having worked its way up through the tarmac with which it was covered in 1951. At least it was visible a couple of weeks ago when I last looked.

Many's the time my long-suffering father waited patiently, letting inferior types go by until a 'Feltham' appeared, and once, changing trams at St Leonard's church at the top of the hill where the 8, 10 and 20 routes met the 16s and 18s, I leapt aboard a Southwark-bound 'Feltham'. The tram immediately set off before Great Aunt Hatt, a lady well into her 60s in whose charge I had been placed, could climb aboard. She pursued us gallantly over the busy road junction, but gradually fell behind, whilst I stood, panic-struck on the platform. I got off at the next stop and we completed the journey, together, in an ex-Walthamstow 'E/1'.

The only other section of track remaining that I am aware of in London from the original tram network is that at the Bloomsbury end of the Kingsway Subway. Others lasted in Beresford Square, Woolwich, until the late 1970s. I wonder if there is anywhere else in London — perhaps tarmacked over — or has every other piece been dug up and sold for its scrap value?

None of the new Croydon Tramlink track follows the 16, 18 or 42 routes, being orientated east-west rather than north-south, although certain sections do operate over erstwhile tram routes abandoned earlier. I have a hazy memory, as a very small child, of seeing a bit of track in Tamworth Road, West Croydon, where trams once again run, beside where I used to poke my nose through the fence and wait for a 'W' class 2-6-4T to come bursting out under the bridge hauling a load of coal for the gas works beyond Wandle Park, along the trackbed the trams now use.

I travelled by tram between January 1946 and July 1948 to Winterbourne Primary School, Norbury, and from September 1948 until the trams were withdrawn in April 1951 to Whitgift Middle School in the heart of Croydon, where the Whitgift Centre now stands. I used sometimes to walk to Winterbourne, especially if I was saving up for the next delivery of Dinky Toys to Wises, along the main road from school. Production had only just restarted after the war and the locals would often beat those of us who lived at a distance to the most sought-after models, the double-deck STL easily topping the list. The schoolboy grapevine worked with such efficiency that I sometimes suspected they were waiting at the counter as the grey cardboard boxes — no fancy coloured individual ones in those days — were delivered.

I was forever being reminded by my parents to beware the hazards of tram lines when out on my bike. Now that track is once again to be found in the streets of Croydon, I expect a new generation of parents is repeating the warning. However, in truth, tram tracks are no more hazardous than drain and manhole covers as well as the myriad other imperfections of the road surface which cyclists soon learn to avoid instinctively and subconsciously.

Once the trams had gone, travelling to and from school was rather less exciting. Few of the replacement RTs were actually new, most being second-hand cast-offs from Wandsworth, and, although the RT was quite the finest double-decker of its generation, there were an awful lot of them and one sometimes longed for a bit of variety. The LTs and STs had all been withdrawn, the STLs were on their way out, and so to vary things I would sometimes catch a 190 (the 42 tram replacement) to Thornton Heath station and then take a train to East Croydon. It being the rush hour I would board one of the very few services which stopped at the down fast platform, a train of four 'NOLs', elderly LSWR-built carriages converted to EMUs in the 1930s and working back to the sidings at Coulsdon North.

If this palled, I might take a 115 bus from the bottom of our road. This was a service that was worked jointly by Croydon RTs and Sutton D class Daimlers. Although we always regarded these latter as rather inferior austerity vehicles, they had, in fact, Park Royal bodies dating from 1946 and were almost of postwar standard, being virtually identical to a batch of Southdown PD1s. They were also contemporary with some London PD1s, with Leyland bodies,

the STD class, and some of these worked the 115 when new, before being transferred to Loughton.

The 115, on its way to its terminus at Croydon Airport, crossed the route of the 630 trolleybus at Mitcham Road, so I would change there and complete my journey thus. It all took a lot longer than a straightforward run down the main London Road and cost double, so I didn't do it very often.

13

Trolleybuses

The replacement of the South London trams by motorbuses signalled the eventual demise of the trolleybus. If the war had not intervened just about all London's tram network would have gone over to trolleybus operation. As it was, when No 1721, the last trolley of prewar design (albeit for South Africa, not London), entered service in October 1941, London's trolleybus fleet was the largest in the world.

Trolleybuses never had an appeal equal to trams', although I wouldn't like any trolleybus enthusiast to over-react to that statement, for the vehicles were interesting enough in their way. Because the trolleybus people of the 1930s had started their careers on the trams, the department kept its distance from the bus people. Liveries, for instance, were different and no tram or trolleybus carried a type prefix — which made spotting rather less interesting. Environmentally, of course, the trolleybus won hands down. There was no pollution and it made practically no noise, although the upper-deck ceiling boomed in a rather intriguing manner as the trolley pole negotiated junctions. The late Poet Laureate, John

◀◀ The routes most associated with the 'Felthams', following their prewar migration from north to south of the river, had been routes 16 and 18, taking them from the Embankment through Croydon almost to the country at Purley. The trams were replaced by buses during the night of 7/8 April 1951; the replacement vehicles operated over route 109. A few days later in this Embankment scene, an RT from Brixton garage (formerly Telford Avenue depot) passes an 'E/3' tram, which has just come through the Kingsway Subway. *D. Sutton/ Ian Allan Library*

◀ Although the South London trams would be replaced by diesel-engined buses, two batches of trolleybuses of Class Q1 were put into service after the war. Built on AEC/BUT chassis, they were an 8ft-wide development of the standard prewar vehicle. A total of 77, including No 1802 seen here, were delivered in 1948 and another identical 50, represented by No 1849 behind, in 1952.

Betjeman, reflected some of the nostalgia for the trolleybus in his lovely poem *Harrow-on-the-Hill*. He wrote of the hissing and clicking of the poles as they slid along the overhead.

The trolleybus was relatively rare south of the Thames as London Transport had concentrated on replacing the trams to the north of the river network. Most of those tram routes to the south of the Thames that had disappeared prewar, largely in the Dartford and Croydon areas, were worked prior to conversion by ancient non-LCC cars which were well past their sell-by date. The outbreak of World War 2 reprieved the remaining trams and, when the southern routes finally went, they were replaced by RT and RTL diesel buses rather than by trolleybuses. The RT and RTL monopoly on these conversions was almost complete, although a few STLs participated in the final conversion programme. There was even one of the early LGOC design 'sit-up-and-beg' variety still in prewar red and white livery.

Although it was not until 1954 that trolleybus conversion became LT policy, the first trolleybus to bus conversion occurred earlier in the decade. As part of the Operation Tramaway conversion programme, on 1 October 1950 the relatively isolated route 612 from Wandsworth to Mitcham was withdrawn and replaced by the new 44 bus route from Mitcham to London Bridge.

The 630, London's second-longest trolleybus route, was operated by Hammersmith depot by 'D' class vehicles and a small number of 'P1s', the very last prewar design trolleys, although they didn't actually appear until 1941. Before my first Ian Allan 'abc' introduced me to the mysteries of the many classes, I divided London's trolleybuses into five varieties. There were the standard ones with squared-off window edges. Then there were the later ones with highly curvaceous and streamlined eyebrows at the front upper deck. The third type was represented by the archaic-looking original LUT 'Diddlers', which I encountered on family expeditions to Hampton Court. Their 1948 replacements — the slightly tubby looking, 8ft-wide BUT 'Q1s' — represented the fourth type. Finally, there were the vehicles that served Croydon's other route, the 654, which was mainly equipped with 'B1s'.

The fate of the London trolleybus network was sealed, on 28 April 1954, by the announcement that, with the exception of the routes in and around Kingston (which would continue to be served by the postwar 'Q1s' until they became life-expired), the whole of the trolleybus fleet would be replaced by buses from January 1958 onwards. In the event, it was not until March 1959 that the conversion programme got under way and, with the sale of the 'Q1s' to Spanish operators, even the token retention of the Kingston routes was not to be. The last London trolleybuses survived into the new decade, being withdrawn in May 1962.

Perhaps the most impressive of all the prewar London bus designs was the final version of the six-wheeled LT, nicknamed the Bluebird. One stands here at Aldgate, ahead of a new RT, shortly before withdrawal in 1949.
A. B. Cross

The Bus Types

The STL and Other Prewar Types

I grew up with the STL, the standard roofbox variety being of exactly the same vintage as myself. The aforementioned 'sit-up-and-beg' STL was so named on account of the fact that this batch had originally been fitted with petrol engines and, when these were replaced by diesel units, the frames had to be raised to accommodate them. It wasn't until 1934 that the standard, graceful curved front evolved and stayed in production with various minor modifications until 1939.

There should have been a smooth transition from STL production to RT but the war frustrated this. As a result, further additions to the STL class arrived during the war years in the shape of unfrozen chassis. These were fitted with a variety of second-hand and austerity bodies, including some lowbridge ones. In 1946, 20 very handsome but totally provincial Weymann-bodied Regents, STL2682-2701, completed the class in theory. However, in May 1950, STL2477 appeared with a completely new experimental body made of prefabricated parts designed by a Chiswick engineer, Arthur Sainsbury.

The STL was the first London bus to appear on the second-hand market in any numbers. World War 2, despite lower maintenance standards, prolonged the life of many buses. This coincided with a slowing down of the hitherto rapid improvement in comfort, performance and appearance that had characterised the first three decades in the history of the motorbus. Fifteen-year-old vehicles were thus not outrageously outdated in the early 1950s, although they might well be pretty tired. My last few journeys in STLs were characterised by shudders and rattling windows, even though many had been refurbished by a variety of bodybuilders and repairers to keep them going until the RT family was in full production. Some second-hand STLs went abroad, others saw further service with small operators in the UK, whilst quite a few were rebodied.

The last standard LTs and STs were withdrawn in January 1950, apart from the single-deck LTs which continued until the summer of 1953 and eight lowbridge STs, some of which continued until 1952. The last prewar STLs and STDs finished passenger service in 1954, outliving the austerity and early postwar Bs, Gs and Ds. The unpopular 'unfrozen' STD class had been the first wartime deliveries to depart from the fleet.

The RF saw off all prewar single-deck buses and Green Line coaches, although the famous 10T10s, pride of the prewar and early postwar Green Line fleet, found work as staff buses for a little while longer.

An astonishing veteran, which was not taken out of use until 1954, was the last NS, other than the preserved NS1995, which of course is still with us. This was one of a group that had been converted to staff canteens in the 1930s. Most had been replaced by 10 purpose-built, Bedford-hauled semi-trailers in the late 1940s, but

◄ The last standard LTs and STs were withdrawn from passenger service at the beginning of 1950. Amongst the final duties of both types was taking part in the special Derby Day service to Epsom Racecourse. Four are seen here, led by ST189, which survived until January 1950. *Roy Marshall*

There remained a need for lowbridge buses and so eight lowbridge STs, quite different in appearance from the standard ST, six of them like ST1089 seen here with Short Bros body, were retained. ST1089, a green Country Area bus all its life, continued to work from Addlestone garage until March 1953. *D. A. Jones*

A rather more modern lowbridge bus is seen here amongst the slush outside Morden station in March 1952. This is STL2229, which was a 1938 bus fitted with its lowbridge body in 1943. It was allocated to Merton Garage for the 127 route. *A. B. Cross*

▲ this single example survived. One of these Bedford semi-trailers is preserved at Cobham.

The 'prewar' RT — none had actually entered service until January 1940 — managed to survive in passenger service beyond 1954 — but only just, for 1955 saw all but seven of them relegated to the training and staff bus fleets, whilst the postwar STDs and STLs were all withdrawn and sold for service elsewhere. The seven 'prewar' RTs still required for passenger service were repainted green and sent to Hertford garage to work the 327 route where a somewhat flimsy bridge precluded the use of the rather heavier postwar RTs. The prewar vehicles lasted until the summer of 1957.

▶ If the RT family was to become the archetypal double-deck bus for London of the 1950s, the equivalent single-deck bus was undoubtedly represented by the RF. Based around the AEC Regal IV, an underfloor-engined chassis first introduced in 1950, the type was to be ordered in huge numbers for both Central and Country Area operation. A total of 700 of the type was ordered by LT for delivery between 1951 and 1953. Of these, the first 25 were 27ft 6in long, whilst the remainder were all built to 30ft length; all were constructed to a width of 7ft 6in although the maximum permitted width had increased to 8ft by this date. The first 25, the 27ft 6in

At the other, South Wimbledon, terminus of the 127 is D4. This is a Duple-bodied Daimler CWA6 of 1944 and was a type more usually associated with the 127 and Merton Garage, which was home to all the Central Area wartime Daimlers, and later Sutton. D4 has just received its last overhaul and has been repainted in the sombre red all-over livery relieved by one cream band separating the lower and upper decks. It was withdrawn in January 1953. *F. G. Reynolds*

A number of STLs were sold by London Transport for further service, but the great majority, and practically all the STs and LTs, went straight for breaking up. Two STLs and an ST await their end in a scrapyard. *A. D. Packer*

19

The first examples of London's postwar single-deck vehicles, the RFs, appeared in 1951. There were 700 in all, AEC Regal Mark IVs with Metro-Cammell bodywork. The first 25 were sightseeing coaches, painted in an attractive Lincoln green and grey livery with red lettering. RF2 is seen here when new in High Holborn with a collection of trolleybuses in the background. *D. A. Jones*

Concurrent with RF production were these half-deckers operated by London Transport for British European Airways. They usually flaunted rather more exotic destinations than this preserved example is offering.

Concurrent with the delivery of the first RFs came the RFWs. These 15 vehicles were true coaches with high-backed seats, 8ft wide and a body design by ECW. RFW5 is seen at Victoria on 19 August 1961 prior to heading off with 39 jolly sightseers for Hampton Court and Windsor.

variety, were originally destined for private hire work, being fitted (in the case of RF1-15) with air-operated door and glass roof panels and (in the case of the remaining 10) with luggage racks. The latter vehicles were ultimately to be transferred to Green Line. Green Line was also to see large numbers of the 30ft model, a number of which were transferred from both Central and Country Area duties.

The arrival of the RFs signalled the end of all prewar single-deck buses and coaches. Longest lived were the handsome Green Line 10T10s of the T-type, a number of which, such as T536, were repainted red and served in the Central Area until 1954.

None of the later prewar Green Line vehicles, nor indeed the RFs, were true coaches as understood by companies such as East Kent, Maidstone & District and Southdown, as the interior of this 10T10 makes abundantly clear. The seats, despite the thicker cushions, are typical bus-style, although the clock hints at a touch of distinction.

Whilst most tram replacement routes were operated by new RTs and RTLs, the final stage used some elderly STLs and prewar RTs. STL822, then 16 years old and officially allocated to the former New Cross depot, loads up on the Embankment ahead of an RTL. *D. A. Jones*

21

A tranquil scene in leafy suburbia. A sparkling SRT154 looks very much at home in Metroland. Do not be deceived; these conversions from STLs with standard RT bodies, introduced in 1949, were a disaster. Underpowered and underbraked, they had all gone by 1954, although their bodies lasted for many more years, remounted on RT chassis. *Ian Allan Library*

There was still work to do for prewar buses withdrawn from passenger service, at least for a brief while. Here STL2428 performs for the TV cameras on the famous Chiswick skidpan in February 1949. I twice had a go on this, as a passenger on the lower deck as one was not allowed upstairs, and very exciting it was. One of the EGO series of STLs, No 2377, is preserved and has been superbly restored at Cobham.
Ian Allan Library

Perhaps more remarkable was the survival of a number of NSs into the postwar era. After the last was withdrawn from passenger service in 1937 some were converted into staff canteens and the former NS429, departmental No 32H, is seen here at Clapham Junction shortly before withdrawal in May 1948 and breaking up at Chiswick.

The RT

I never fail to be astonished every time I encounter a preserved RT by the sheer quality of this classic bus. RT1 took up work in 1939. Thirty years before that one could still ride horsebuses in London. Thirty years later there were still plenty of RTs at work, and production of the type's successor, the Routemaster, which was certainly no more comfortable, had finished; the generation of single-deck types just arriving was mechanically a disaster and the one-person-operated double-deck designs yet to come — the DMS, the Metrobus and the Titan — were not, even when new, as well made and as well appointed as the RT.

RT402, when it went into service from Leyton Garage on 10 May 1947, created a sensation. It had 151 predecessors, the prewar RTs, although only RT1 actually entered passenger service before the outbreak of war, but these were unknown exotica to most Londoners unless you happened to live on any of the Putney-based routes which they frequented. Now the RT type was going to become London's standard, to be seen on practically every trunk road, suburban estate and Home Counties high street served by London's red or green double-deck buses. AEC, as befitted tradition, would supply the chassis, but Chiswick Works was fully occupied with maintenance and so Park Royal and Weymann were contracted to build the bodies. Such would be the demand for new buses throughout the world in the late 1940s and early 1950s that these firms would not be able to supply all that London needed. As a result, Leyland would be asked to build some of the chassis, whilst Metro-Cammell, Leyland, Saunders and Cravens would construct a number of bodies.

Production of the RT ended late in 1954, the highest-numbered being RT4825. The Leyland version, the RTL, ended production around the same time, the last delivered and the highest-numbered, RTL1631, arriving in November. This year, however, was not the last year in which new RTs and RTLs actually went into service. London Transport had over-estimated its needs, the new towns had not grown quite as fast as anticipated, and car ownership was going up by leaps and bounds. All the prewar buses had gone from passenger service by the end of 1954, despite which a number of new RTs and RTLs went straight into store. It was not until much later in the decade that these vehicles were placed in service.

Some enthusiasts felt that an unrelieved diet of RTs, RTLs, RTWs and RFs made the London bus scene altogether too boring. There were a few exceptions, like the lowbridge RLHs — essentially standard provincial vehicles — and the cute little Country Area GSs, but these were so few they hardly counted.

◄ The classic RT-type interior. This is actually the lower deck of an RTW, but so well had Leyland adapted its usual PD2 chassis that the bodywork is standard London Transport in every respect.

▼ Full indicator blinds were restored in 1950, about the same time as all-over red or green, save for a pale cream band between the decks, became the standard livery. RT3847 and RT3849 demonstrate the old and the new style in this 1950 view. *Ian Allan Library*

For a little while it was possible to see buses with full indicator blinds and cream upper-deck window surrounds, a condition that most effectively displayed the RT type's handsome lines. Here RT1660 is pictured heading south across Tower Bridge on route 78 towards Dulwich. *London Transport*

How to lift an RT by hand. This picture was taken in Palmers Green garage to demonstrate the Lansing Bagnall hydraulic lift, but is of interest to us in that it shows just how an RT could sparkle on completion of overhaul, emerging as, in effect, a brand-new bus. Weymann-bodied RT443 has just been overhauled for the first time. In the background is an RT that still retains its upper-deck cream window surrounds, whilst on the right another all-red early roofbox example is being attended to. Note the reflection of the photographer's flash in the windscreen of RT443. *Ian Allan Library*

RT and RTL chassis undergoing overhaul at Aldenham Works.

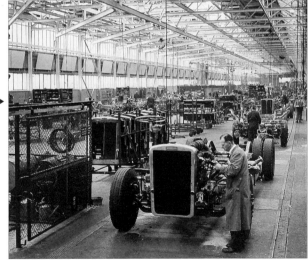

From 1955 the overhaul system at Aldenham resulted in roof box bodies appearing on later chassis — even if the fleet number actually had no connection with that originally allocated to either chassis or body. On the left, RT992, delivered in October 1948, still has an original RT10-type body whilst beside it RT3617, of November 1952, has the earliest style of RT3-type body. The location of this view is alongside Kingston railway station.

An example of a later body on a chassis that had originally carried a roof number box body is RT608 of Dunton Green garage. The bus is seen here at Reeves Corner, Croydon, on its way from Wallington to Tonbridge. This had been one of the original batch of Country Area RTs, delivered to Hemel Hempstead in July 1948.

Newly overhauled RT1025 has retained a RT3/1-type body. Delivered to Epping in November 1948, it is seen working from Windsor garage with the 'winking ear' trafficators that were fitted at the end of the 1950s.

▲ Yet for the true enthusiast London could never be boring. There were all sorts of variations within the RT theme. For instance, we spotters were almost delirious with excitement when the first non-roofbox members appeared. Elmers End garage put its shiny new '8xx' series on the 12 and 194 routes — the latter being a route I used regularly — and Croydon received Nos 1135-1148 and very decently ran them past the top of our road on the 166 and the 166A. All had 'JXN' registrations and my school friends and I quickly learned them off by heart. As a result, we knew instantly the fleet number of any 'JXN' and the earlier 'JXC', 'HLX' and 'HLW' series by looking at the registration numbers — which ought to have done wonders for my school mathematics but didn't seem to have any noticeable effect.

The RTW

The RTW was one of the most distinctive of all London buses, for not only was it the first 8ft-wide motorbus, but it was entirely Leyland built — chassis, engine and body. The Leyland engineers adapted the standard provincial PD2 chassis so that the RTW body was six inches wider than the Park Royal and Weymann version fitted to the great majority of RTs and RTLs.

The RTW began work in the suburbs as the Metropolitan Police were convinced that the extra six inches would bring traffic in Central London to a shuddering halt. To the Metropolitan Police's amazement, a trial with as many RTWs as London Transport could muster in 1951 proved perfectly satisfactory and so, for the rest of its career, the class became associated with some of London's most famous routes — including the 8, the 11, the 15 and the 74 — becoming a familiar sight in the West End and the City. The class had worked into Croydon, when new, from Bromley garage on the 119, and, in the twilight of their careers they returned, on the 109 from Brixton, the very last London garage to operate the class.

It was at this time — 1965 — that I came across a group of RTWs parked in a station yard at Southport. As such, they formed a contrast with the standard all-Leyland PD2 in Ribble cherry red livery, the usual fare in that part of the world. When their London days were over, numerous RTWs were exported in large numbers to Ceylon (now Sri Lanka) and elsewhere far away, but eight survive in various states of repair and preservation in the UK.

Although a few RTLs were painted green and worked briefly in the Country Area, the RTW was always a Central Area bus.

The GS

Although much of the Country Area route network was operated by standard bus and coach designs, there were a number of routes where the level of traffic demanded vehicles that were much smaller in capacity terms. The ill-assorted collection of of10 very small single-deck buses was steadily replaced by Chiswick-designed vehicles.

From the 1930s and until the 1960s there was a need for a small capacity one-man single-deck vehicle to work some of the marginally viable rural runs where a full-sized bus was either not needed or could not be operated. The Leyland Cub had been doing this since 1935, but by the 1950s this type was increasingly life-expired. Its replacement was a bus designed by a committee which should therefore neither have looked right nor performed very well. In fact the 26-seat GS type of 1953 with its Guy chassis, Perkins engine, Fordson lorry front end and ECW body with RF-type rear end was an admirable little bus. If many of its 84 members served less than their allotted span with London Transport this was because of changing economic conditions and they were snapped up on the second-hand market.

In the Country Area there were certain routes where the RF was considered unsuitable and so a 26-seat replacement for the Leyland Cub was ordered. The result was the normal-control GS class. Based on the Guy Vixen chassis, it had a Fordson front end and a body by ECW that combined London Transport and ECW features. Amongst the latter was the first regular use of slide-vent windows, visually less appealing and in use less satisfactory than London's standard wind-down ones but presumably cheaper. Overall the little GS was an appealing vehicle. GS3 of Hitchin garage poses with five rather self-conscious passengers. *London Transport*

Another suburban bus, although not for long, was the RTW. The Metropolitan Police looked askance when asked to allow these adventurous 8ft-wide all-Leylands to operate in central London upon their introduction in 1949. However, a year later the police relented, hence RTW179 seen here on the 14A. *J. H. Aston*

▾ The RLH

Another non-standard vehicle was the RLH. There was much speculation concerning London's standard postwar lowbridge bus. Some lowbridge STL bodies had been built during the war, but otherwise the few routes so restricted had made do with an odd collection of austerity Daimlers and pre-London Transport STs and STLs. There might well have been a lowbridge RT but, as it happened, a batch of 20 Weymann-bodied Regent IIIs originally intended for Midland General became available in 1950 and

London Transport decided upon this option. Another 56 arrived in 1952. They worked in both Central and Country areas. Although the chassis and engine had much in common with the RT, the RLHs were of totally provincial design in just about every respect, including a one-piece indicator at the front and nothing other than a stencil at the back. Rather surprisingly the last RLHs continued in service into the Merlin era; these new single-deck vehicles could carry more passengers on their one deck than the RLH could on its awkwardly-seated two.

◄ There was a considerably greater proportion of single-deck vehicles in the Country Area fleet. The revolutionary AEC Q class served as Central and Country Area buses and Green Line coaches. Green Q7, fitted with a BRCW 35-seat bus body of 1935, is seen at one of the southern extremities of the London Transport area in East Grinstead ahead of a Southdown Leyland TS7 bus bound for Brighton.

Country Area Buses

We will end this look at the London scene with a few words about the vast outer-suburban area, the rural reaches and Home Counties towns covered by the buses and coaches of the Country Area. Although AECs dominated the fleet, Leyland made its presence felt, particularly with a number of far-from-standard single-deck designs and Green Line coaches introduced in the late 1930s.

Before the coming of the RT, the standard Country Area double-deck type was the STL. Two series of the Country Area version of the standard Chiswick design had been put into service by London Transport, the chief difference being that these vehicles had front entrances. There seemed little logic for this departure from Central Area practice; presumably they were based on the 'Godstone' front-entrance STLs, standard provincial Weymann-bodied lowbridge

Regents which worked the 410 from Godstone garage. These had sliding doors and had proved popular with passengers. However, the sliding doors were omitted from the standard version, which completely negated the whole idea as the wind whistled in — no heaters in those days — and the layout meant there were fewer seats than in rear-entrance buses. Despite this they were a great novelty to a lad familiar with rear-entrance buses, and a number of garages operated them on Croydon routes. Later on, many Central Area STLs of various types were sent out to sample rural life, some without being painted green.

STs were also found in the Country Area, although the last green ones disappeared from Croydon when a batch of unfrozen 'FXT'-registered STLs took up work from Godstone on the 409 and the 411 in the early 1940s. Excursions to Reigate brought us into Q

territory, that remarkably advanced AEC design with the engine
placed amidships. London bought far more Qs than all other
operators put together and they formed a large proportion of the
prewar single-deck fleet, being used in both the Central and Country
areas and in the Green Line fleet. Equally advanced was the
underfloor-engined TF, a Leyland design which came out just before
the war, but which didn't really make the most of its layout as it was
fitted with a half cab. The TFs joined the Green Line fleet, along with
the Qs, but the mainstay of this operation was the splendid 10T10.
This class of 255 Regals came out in 1938 and 1939.

Yet another revolutionary single-decker used primarily in the
Country Area was the CR. This was a rear-engined version of the
Leyland Cub. The normal-control Cub featured in both red and
green fleets and was highly successful, eventually being replaced in
the early 1950s by the GS. The GS was an ECW-bodied Guy, and
represented London's last normal-control design. However, the CR
was a bit too revolutionary for it was withdrawn within a few
months of entering service, its limited capacity and mechanical
uncertainties being of little use in wartime conditions. The class
reappeared after the war in various roles, but it remained unreliable.

I came across several stored in Reigate garage, awaiting a recall to service which never came.

The STL and the 10T10 types provided virtually the entire green presence in Croydon until 1949. Then a veritable flood of RT deliveries to Dunton Green, Chelsham, Godstone, East Grinstead, Reigate, Leatherhead, Dorking and Guildford garages all but wiped out the STL as far as the streets of Croydon were concerned. However, examples remained in rapidly diminishing numbers elsewhere. Rumour had it that STLs were still to be found in the Gerrards Cross area in 1953, so, greatly daring, I headed off in a Green Line RF — this type having taken over from the 10T10s — to this unknown territory far away in the frozen north. The rumours turned out to be just that — nothing but RFs and RTs were visible — so just to get my own back I returned by train to Marylebone, where LNER-designed Class L1 2-6-4Ts had also established a similar monopoly.

Monopoly or not, I had to admit that the 1949/50 green RTs when new, still with cream upper-deck window surrounds, looked most handsome and Chelsham garage became a favourite haunt as many of the batch numbered RT2499-2521 were allocated there. Later, in 1950, green (or red) all-over became standard apart from the cream waistband. This did nothing to brighten up things in the dour years of postwar austerity.

The Routemaster

The Routemaster was designed to replace the trolleybus and it is true to say that more research and experimentation went into this bus than any other in London's history. The first, RM1, made its initial public appearance at the 1954 Commercial Motor Show. With a tiny provincial-type route indicator — allegedly in the interests of weight saving — and a 'tin front', it did not impress everyone. Moreover, its seating capacity was not as great as that of the standard London trolleybus. Three further prototypes followed, one of them being a Leyland-engined, ECW-bodied, Green Line coach. It would be June 1959 before the well-proportioned production RM began work in London, and November of that year when they first replaced trolleybuses, from Poplar and West Ham in the East End. By this date the revolutionary rear-engined Leyland Atlantean, with a seating capacity of up to 78, was in full production. The Routemaster — with its open rear platform, half cab and 64-seat capacity — seemed to belong to an earlier generation. However, its superb engineering, combined with a body

that could be stretched to accommodate 72 seats, has proved it to be ▲ an almost timeless design, ideal for central London conditions. The success of the design is such that, 45 years after the prototype was first unveiled and some 30 years after the last came off the AEC production line, almost 600 remain in service. Apparently anachronistic when entering service in large numbers, the timelessness of the Routemaster design is such that it has become an almost universal image of London worldwide.

Two Country Area RTs, Nos 2509 and 2510 of Chelsham garage, pausing in St Michael's Road, West Croydon, demonstrate the uniquely informative and perfectly aligned 'via' and destination information offered by the RT family in the 1950s. The date is 21 May 1956.

RTs replaced Ds and STLs on the heavily trafficked East London Green Line routes out of Aldgate. Although a standard bus in most respects (except livery), the RT type was ideal for the task. RT3258 speeds along the Romford Road past a Bedford OB/ Duple Vista on 25 August 1950.
R. E. Vincent

▲ A rare prewar trolleybus colour picture. Nos 115 and 103, two of the short-wheelbase 'B2' class 60-seaters, delivered new to Bexleyheath depot in the winter of 1935, are seen against a typically industrial Southeast London background at the Woolwich terminus of the 696 and 698 routes in March 1938. The red-painted mudguards and silver roofs disappeared in the 1940s; otherwise the livery of London's trolleybuses changed very little throughout their careers. *C. S. Perrier collection/Colour-Rail (LT103)*

Sandwiched between the Houses of Parliament on the north bank of the Thames and Lambeth Palace on the south bank, 'E/1r' No 1763 heads along Lambeth Palace Road in October 1949 on route 26. The 'Rehabilitated' 'E/1s' emerged during the 1930s with flush side panels. In the immediate postwar years, LT overhauled and repainted a large number of trams in order to keep the fleet operational until the policy of conversion could be recommenced. Route 26, from Clapham Junction to Borough, was operated from Wandsworth and Clapham depots, with the former providing 'E/3s' and the latter 'E/1s' for the service. The route was one of the casualties of the first stage of 'Operation Tramaway' on 30 September/1 October 1950.
W. E. Robertson/
Colour-Rail (LT122)

By the summer of 1940, although a number of services ran along the Embankment and others terminated at Southwark and Battersea Bridges and Victoria, it was only the three Kingsway Subway services, Nos 31/3/5, which could truly be called North London ones. 'E/3' No 1962 emerges from the subway on its way to Islington Green whilst STL1862 lurks in the shadows on its way from South Croydon to Chalk Farm in October 1949. The tram would actuallyt outlast the STL, the latter being withdrawn in August of the following year whilst the 'E/3' wasn't broken up until October 1952.
W. E. Robertson/Colour-Rail (LT123)

This is a view of North End, Croydon, on 1 September 1945, opposite the Whitgift Almshouses at the junction of George Street and Crown Hill. An 'E/3' tram, No 1910, is working the local 42 route and stands beside STL255 with a number of boarded up, bomb-blasted windows. The flags fly over Allders' department store marking the end of World War 2 15 days earlier. Both this and the previous illustration were taken by Harold Bennett, a professional photographer, who lived in Sanderstead. I think we can safely claim that these are the only London Transport pictures taken on a film bought in Medicine Hat, Alberta! Harold had been working there earlier as a flying instructor with the RAF. His camera was a Leica 111b, the film Kodachrome 35mm. *Harold Bennett*

A lady with flowing skirt has just alighted from a spruce-looking No 489, a 'B1' class short-wheelbase trolleybus, near Norwood Junction. This batch of five BRCW-bodied Leyland vehicles was delivered in September 1936, following the main batch of 30 a few months earlier. The 654 was one of two trolleybus routes that served Croydon. *J. Copland/Photobus*

Croydon's other trolleybus route was the 630 from Harlesden to West Croydon (where it provided the only physical link with the otherwise isolated route 654), at just over 14 miles, the second-longest in London. Here another BRCW-bodied Leyland, this time a long-wheelbase 70-seat 'D3' of 1937, No 511 based at Hammersmith depot, appears in immaculate condition. *J. Copland/Photobus*

In the years immediately after the war London Transport bought new buses virtually wherever it could. Few could have been described as standard. Mann Egerton had not previously supplied bodies for new London buses but 130 single-deck ones were built in 1948/9. Of these, 30 were painted green, mounted on AEC Regal chassis and put into the T class, whilst the others, minus the sliding entrance door, became the Central Area's Leyland TD class. TD128 is seen here working from Kingston, which was a garage long associated with single-deck vehicles. *Geoffrey Morant/Photobus*

The earliest postwar RTs continued the prewar RT and later STL design feature of mounting the front route number indicator in the roof. Saunders Engineering, based on the Isle of Anglesey, built 300 of these, RT4267, delivered in February 1951, being the very last roofbox-design body built for London Transport. RT3186, seen here working from Merton Garage, was originally a green bus based at High Wycombe but on overhaul was fitted with a Saunders body. No Saunders bodies were ever painted green in LT service.
Arnold Richardson/Photobus

The first production Leyland version of the RT, the RTL, took up work in London just before Christmas 1948. Park Royal-bodied RTL437, seen here in the familiar surroundings of Victoria bus station, was one of a batch delivered to the west London garage of Hanwell in November 1949, where they replaced STLs on the suburban 55 route. By the time this picture was taken it had moved right across London to Barking and regularly worked through the fashionable heart of the West End. RTL437 was to survive almost exactly two decades in LT service, being sold to a dealer in Yorkshire for scrap in May 1969. Numerous others were to be sold for export, with many ending up in Ceylon.
Arnold Richardson/Photobus

Although it is not the first time this picture has been published, no book portraying London in colour in the years immediately after World War 2 could possibly omit this wonderful evocation of the capital and the trams that served it so well. 'Feltham' No 2153 on route 16 follows an 'E/3' across Westminster Bridge whilst another 'E/3' is approaching on the southbound track in October 1949. *W. E. Robertson/ Colour-Rail (LT125)*

An 'E/1' swings off the Embankment and into the autumn sun as it heads towards Westminster Bridge, followed by two 'E/3s' in October 1951.
W. E. Robertson/ Colour-Rail (LT117)

The four-track Dog Kennel Hill section in Dulwich is pictured during October 1949. One of the LCC cars built especially for heavily graded routes, 'HR/2' No 105 has just stopped to allow a mother and child to alight. In the distance another 'HR/2' is beginning its ascent. As many of the 'HR/2s' worked only on conduit routes they were not fitted with trolley poles. The four-motor 'HR/2' trams, built by Hurst Nelson in 1929/30, had dominated the Dog Kennel Hill routes for many years. The four-track layout on the 1 in 11 gradient had been adopted in 1912 in order that no two trams would be on the hill on the same track at the same time. The Dog Kennel Hill routes were amongst those that were to be converted to bus operation on the night of 6/7 October 1951 as Stage 5 of 'Operation Tramaway'. The trolley-pole-fitted members of the 'HR/2' class were transferred to New Cross depot whilst those without were transferred to operate over route 35 through the Kingsway Subway. *W. E. Robertson/Colour Rail (LT154)*

Nelson Road, Greenwich, pictured in October 1949: the shabby surroundings are far removed from the tourist-orientated image of Greenwich 50 years on. 'E/1' No 1219 on route 70 is passing one of the same class modernised by London Transport in the 1930s. The two routes to Greenwich Church — the 68 from Waterloo and the 70 from Tooley Street — were destined to be replaced by buses as Stage 4 of 'Operation Tramaway' on the night of 10/11 July 1951. This was the smallest of the stages in the conversion of the south London tramway network to bus operation. *W. E. Robertson/Colour Rail (LT115)*

The 29 was the last route to be allocated a full complement of outside-staircase LTs. However, RTs sent them to the scrapheap in 1948 and one of their successors, RT2068, is seen, followed by another RT, at Palmers Green on a Sunday working on 18 August 1968. *Hugh D. Ramsey*

Once the Green Line fleet had been modernised it was the turn of the Central Area. RF387, delivered in December 1952, is seen helping out in the Country Area at South Park, Holmesdale, en route to Redhill in early 1967. *Roy Hobbs*

Although the RT was, like the RF, quite certainly a bus, both were classified as coaches when allocated to Green Line work. RFs were fitted with deeper seat cushions and luggage racks but RTs, such as RT605 seen here working the 719 from Garston garage, were unchanged except for a revised livery and interior heaters, the latter becoming standard on all RTs in later years. *Alastair Douglas/ Photobus*

The RLH was a provincial design of AEC Regent III, which differed from the standard London Regent III in a number of ways. Most notably, the radiator on the RLH was taller and there was a bulge on the side of the bonnet (that housed the dynamo, which was driven by the engine rather than by a propeller shaft). This is RLH36, one of 76 of these Weymann-bodied vehicles delivered in 1950/2. The RLH class represented the only lowbridge double-deckers in the fleet. RLH36 was one of 17 of the type that were transferred to London Country ownership, but they were destined not to survive long. *Arnold Richardson/Photobus*

49

The final 23 RLHs were painted red for Central Area service. Over the years there were transfers and repaints, RLH29, seen here in the City of London at Farringdon station on 28 August 1964, was originally green but had been repainted red and transferred to Dalston garage.
Hugh D. Ramsey

A total of 84 of the attractive little 26-seat, normal-control, ECW-bodied Guy Vixens entered Country Area service in 1953/4. GS20 is seen passing Windsor Castle. A combination of factors — a shift to larger (RF) vehicles and the curtailment of routes — led to the withdrawal of the type relatively early. A number (but not GS20) survive in preservation.
Alastair Douglas/Photobus

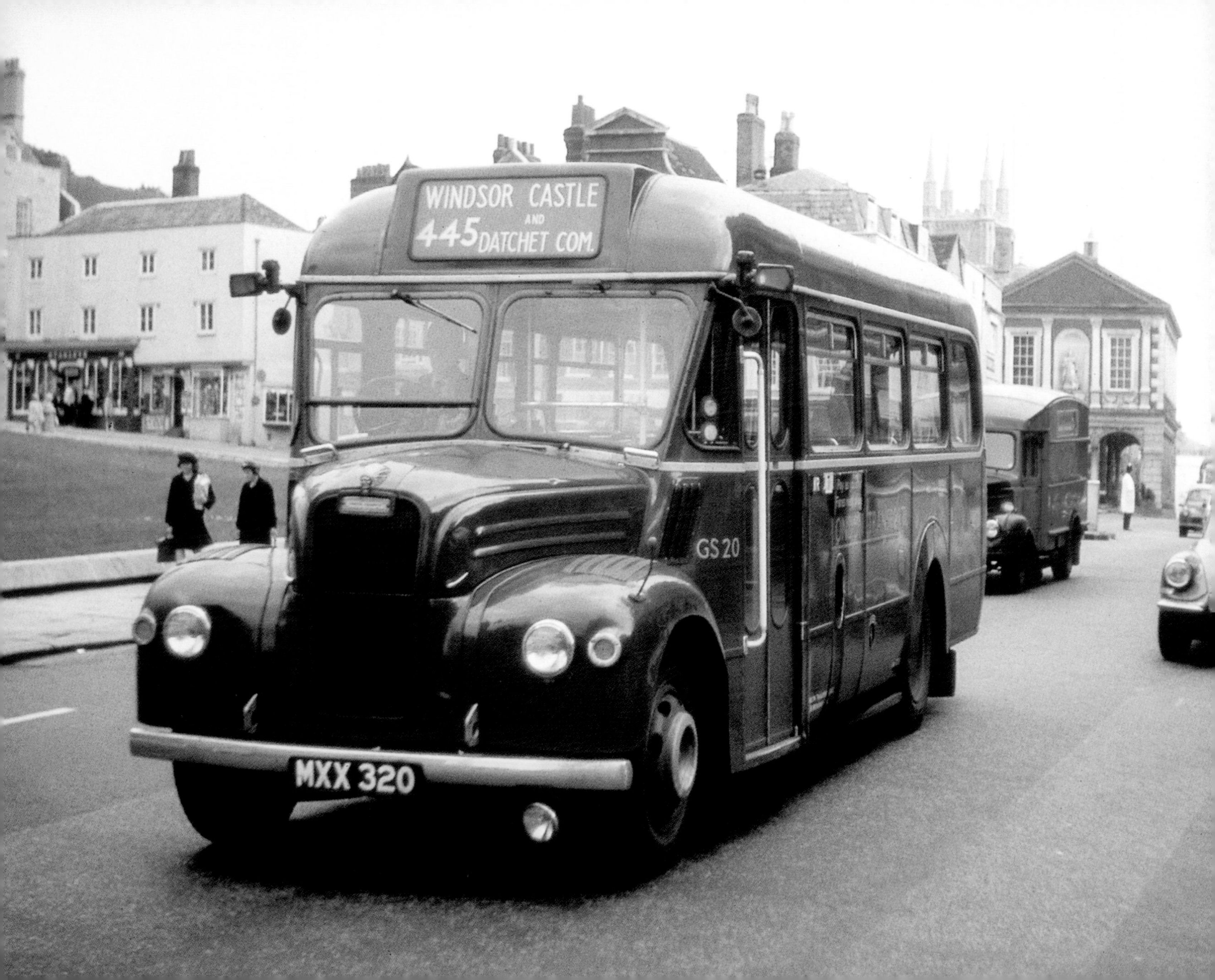
WINDSOR CASTLE
AND
445 DATCHET COM.
GS 20
MXX 320

RF607, new in June 1953 and based at Hertford, approaches its destination on its run from Bishop's Stortford, the most northeasterly point served by London Transport. Behind is a Routemaster coach on the 716 from Hitchin to Chertsey, and behind that an RT. *Alastair Douglas/Photobus*

A trio of trolleybuses — Nos 699, 715 and an unidentified example — stand resplendent at the Uxbridge turning circle of the 607 route from Shepherds Bush in June 1959. One of the routes inherited from London United Tramways, the 607 was introduced with the conversion of the erstwhile tram route in November 1936. The route was traditionally associated with the 'F1' class based at Hanwell depot, and many of this class were to succumb when routes 607 and 655 were converted to RM operation on 8/9 November 1960. *C. Hogg/Colour-Rail (LT158)*

How the times change. In the near 40 years since this view was taken, the level of traffic has grown so dramatically that cars and other road vehicles now outnumber PSVs by a significant margin. In March 1961, when this view of Stamford Hill was taken, trolleybuses outnumber private cars by three to one. Closest trolleybus to the camera is 'P1' class No 1712, heading into the City on route 649 to Liverpool Street. The 649 route ran from Liverpool Street to Waltham Forest and was converted from tram route 49 to trolleybus operation on 16 October 1938. It was to be converted to RM operation on 18/19 July 1961. The 25 members of the 'P1' class had Leyland chassis with MCW bodywork, being delivered in 1941. *J. S. Laker/Colour-Rail (LT170)*

London Transport invested in two batches of trolleybuses in the immediate postwar years. A total of 127 were built, the first 77 in 1948 and the remaining 50 four years later. Classified 'Q1', these 8ft-wide Metro-Cammell-bodied BUTs spent their London careers based at Hanwell, Isleworth and Fulwell depots. No 1860, one of the 1952 batch, is seen working from Hanwell at the Uxbridge terminus of the 607 behind No 730, an all-Leyland 'F1', in 1959. Although 15 years older, the latter is in as near the same perfect condition as the 'Q1'. The family likeness, give or take a few curves, and a bit more width, is striking. *J. S. Laker/Colour-Rail (LT172)*

All-Leyland 'K1' class No 1117 of 1939 is pictured at Hounslow in March 1962. The 657 was one of LT's last seven trolleybus routes and was destined to survive until the final closure in May 1962. Running from Shepherds Bush to Hounslow, the route's origins lay in one of the ex-London United Tramways' tram routes that had been converted to trolleybus operation in October 1935. *J. S. Laker/Colour-Rail (LT211)*

Despite the seemingly excellent condition of London's trolleybus fleet, 4 March 1959 marked the beginning of its end. On that day Bexleyheath and Carshalton depots gave up their trolleybuses and became bus garages. Most Bexleyheath vehicles were broken up at Charlton, the only ones so treated. The others met their end at Colindale. Bexleyheath operated a number of rebuilt and rebodied vehicles, a result of the bombing raid on the depot in June 1944. One of these meets a fiery end whilst another, identified by a painted '97C', stripped of everything reusable, awaits its turn. No 97 was one of the 'B2' class trolleybuses damaged by a 'V1' flying bomb on Bexleyheath depot on 29 June 1944; it was rebodied by NCB in February 1946. Of the 84 vehicles present in the depot when the 'V1' landed, 12 were totally destroyed whilst another 26 had their bodies written off.

RM522 was delivered in November 1960 to Hanwell to replace trolleybuses from that depot but is seen here on Winchmore Hill on 18 August 1968 working the 269 route, one of six trolleybus replacement routes introduced in April 1961.
Hugh D. Ramsey

The Odeon, Finchley, was a favourite gathering place for trolleybuses. Vehicles on routes 517, 617, 521, 621 and 660 terminated there, whilst those on the 609 and the 645 passed by. A lone Routemaster is surrounded by four trolleybuses on 4 November 1961, four days before Routemasters were destined to replace all but the 645 and the 660. *Hugh D. Ramsey*

Class L3 No 1517 heads a line-up of trolleybuses inside Finchley depot on 4 November 1961. The 'L3s' represented the largest class of chassisless trolleybuses to operate in London. Supplied by MCW and fitted with AEC running units and Metrovick motors and controllers, a total of 150 (Nos 1380-1529) were constructed. Two, Nos 1500 and 1515, were fitted with automatic acceleration when new. *Hugh D. Ramsey*

Class N1 No 1633 is pictured at the Tally Ho!, North Finchley, on 4 November 1961 as it heads south for Hammersmith on the 660. *Hugh D. Ramsey*

61

I well remember the heavy snowfalls that greeted 1962. During the afternoon of 3 January, the last day of the 645, 660, 662 and 666 routes, the sun broke through and is seen here shining on 'L3s' Nos 1451 and 1461 in Regent's Park Road, Finchley.
A. G. Forsyth/Colour-Rail (LT166)

Hanwell garage is recorded in September 1960 with trolleybuses alongside an exquisite prewar Ford and a Morris Minor. On the extreme left is 'F1' No 737, whilst in the centre is 'Q1' No 1880, which was shortly to be exported. Alongside No 1880 is another 'Q1', No 1768, which was to become the example of the type to be preserved by London Transport and today forms part of the London Transport Museum collection.
J. S. Laker/Colour-Rail (LT174)

◀◀ Pictured in April 1957, London Transport 0-6-0ST No L53 is seen at Neasden power station. Neasden was one of a number of electricity-generating stations constructed to provide power to the newly electrified lines in and around London at the turn of the century. In Neasden's case, the power station was built on the orders of the Metropolitan Railway between 1902 and 1904. Electric services using power generated at Neasden commenced on 1 January 1905. *L. V. Reason/ Colour-Rail (LT137)*

◀ Also recorded at Neasden during April 1957 was this close-up of No L53 with a member of its crew standing alongside. Built by Peckett in 1897 (Works No 664), the locomotive was one of two Peckett 0-6-0STs owned by the Metropolitan Railway and was originally No 101. Sister locomotive No 102 was delivered in 1899 (Works No 823). *L. V. Reason/ Colour-Rail (LT136)*

In order to supplement its steam locomotive fleet, London Transport acquired a number of ex-GWR pannier tanks. Between October 1956 and July 1963, 13 locomotives were taken over. In November 1959 No L91 brings a crane down past Raans Crossing at Amersham Common. No L91 was originally GWR No 5752 and was one of the first two locomotives to arrive, being transferred in February 1957 to replace one of the surviving ex-Metropolitan Railway 0-4-4T 'E' class locomotives. No L91 was destined to have only a short career on London Transport, being withdrawn in November 1960.
The late J. P. Mullett/ Colour-Rail (LT40)

Pictured in 1958 at the Lillie Bridge coal stage, 0-6-0T No L31 has been cleaned to an immaculate standard. Built by Hunslet in 1930, No L31 was one of two delivered to the District Railway. It and sister locomotive No L30 were both to survive until the early 1960s. *Colour-Rail (LT101)*

In April 1959 a very mixed rake of stock is pictured departing from Plaistow with a District Line service to Wimbledon. *Trevor B. Owen/Colour-Rail (LT31)*

In 1922/3 the Metropolitan Railway replaced its existing electric locomotives with a batch of 20 constructed by Metropolitan-Vickers. The new locomotives utilised parts from the original 1906 locomotives and were destined to provide the motive power for the Metropolitan's long-distance services for nearly 40 years. Today, two of the class survive: No 5 in the London Transport Museum and No 12 retained by the Underground. Pictured whilst in service, No 7 *Edmund Burke* arrives at Baker Street in 1959. *J. G. Dewing/Colour-Rail (LT6)*

Looking immaculate having been freshly repainted, a rake of 1938 stock stands outside Oakwood depot in February 1954. The 1938 stock, which numbered some 1,121 cars, was the result of the construction of four experimental rakes built by Metropolitan-Cammell in the mid-1930s. Three of these rakes were streamlined, but the relatively low speeds attained by Underground stock made such an innovation meaningless and the fourth rake had a flatter front end. It was this rake that set the pattern for the production vehicles, which were produced by Metro-Cammell itself and by Birmingham RC&W. The 1938 stock was used on the Bakerloo and Northern lines almost exclusively for the period covered in this book, with some also running on the Piccadilly Line. *Colour-Rail (LT142)*

Looking resplendent, despite being in the autumn of its operational career, Class L3 No 1526 heads past the Raynes Park Hotel en route to Wimbledon on the 604. The 604, running from Hampton Court to Wimbledon, was one of the routes centred around Kingston which, if the original LT plans had come to fruition, would have survived well into the 1960s. However, the sale of the 'Q1s' to Spain brought this scheme to an end and the 604, along with the other remaining London trolleybus routes, was converted to bus operation on 8/9 May 1962. The 604 had one of the longest trolleybus histories in London, being converted by the London United Tramways (as route 4 replacing tram route 71) on 2 September 1931.
Geoffrey Morant/Photobus

Two trolleybuses, led by 'Q1' 1790, stand at Hayes End on route 607. London's only postwar trolleybus deliveries, the 'Q1' class totalled 127, being delivered between February 1948 and December 1952. Chassis were supplied by BUT with bodywork by MCCW. At the date of this photograph, No 1790 was allocated to Hanwell (HL) garage. This depot was to retain an allocation of trolleybuses until 8 November 1960. The bulk of the 'Q1s', including No 1790 (which went to Pontevedra), were sold to Spanish operators.
Geoffrey Morant/Photobus

Class B1 No 87 is seen at Crystal Palace on the 654 route to Sutton. The 654 was largely isolated, being one of the relatively few trolleybus routes in south London. The 654 had been converted to trolleybus operation from Sutton to West Croydon — where it made its one physical connection with the rest of the network (0.8 miles of common wiring with the 630) — on 8 December 1935 and extended thence to Crystal Palace on 9 February 1936. One factor in the decision to make conversion of the 654 to bus operation part of the first stage of the trolleybus abandonment programme — on 3/4 March 1959 — was the age (23 years) of the 'B1' class trolleybuses.
Geoffrey Morant/Photobus

Pictured at West Croydon on the 630, No 1700 was another of the wartime 'P1' class. Running from Harlesden to West Croydon — where it met the 654 — the 630 route was almost the longest trolleybus service operated by London Transport. At some 14.5 miles, it was exceeded in length only by the 14.8-mile route 655. It was converted to trolleybus operation on 12 September 1937 and was converted to RM operation (as route 220) on 19/20 July 1960. A single journey over the 630 took some 77min. *Geoffrey Morant/Photobus*

Pictured at Fulwell depot on the last day of service, 8 May 1962, Class L3 No 1524 heads towards Hampton Court with a service on route 667. Part of the route involved running to Hammersmith from Young's Corner; this and the section from Young's Corner to Shepherds Bush represented parts of London's first electric tram routes — opening in April 1901 — and thus had a history of some 61 years of electric operation when the trolleybuses were withdrawn. Sister 'L3' No 1521 had the honour of being the last London trolleybus to operate in public service. It was subsequently to pass into preservation via the scrap merchant George Cohen. *Geoffrey Morant/Photobus*

At a distance of 40 years it seems inconceivable that a dual carriageway would carry as little traffic as this, but when 'F1' No 724 was recorded running towards Acton Vale on the 607 only a van and a small lorry shared the road with it. The 100 members of the all-Leyland 'F1' class were delivered in 1937, with the first arriving in the March of that year. The vehicles were allocated to Hanwell, where they replaced the earlier 'D2' type. The vast majority of the type survived at Hanwell until the 607 and 655 routes were converted to bus operation on 8/9 November 1960. *Geoffrey Morant/Photobus*

In total, some 52 members of the 'C1' class were delivered in 1935. Of these, the first 10 were delivered with Weymann bodies, whilst the balance had bodies from Metro-Cammell-Weymann; all were built on AEC 664T chassis. Here one of the class, No 159, is pictured running on the 613 route towards Hampstead. The 613 and 513 were parallel routes, but operating in opposite directions between Hampstead and Parliament Hill Fields via Holborn. The tram routes were converted to trolleybus operation on 10 July 1938 and were to survive until 31 January/1 February 1961, when RMs, operating on routes 45 and 63, took over. *J. Copland/Photobus*

Pictured at Hayes End on an in-bound 607 to Shepherds Bush, Class 'K1' No 1152 is captured amidst the traffic. The 150-strong all-Leyland 'K1s' — Nos 1055-1154 and 1255-1304 — were delivered in 1938/9. The 'K1s' and 'K2s (Nos 1155-1254 and 1305-54) both had Metrovick electrical motors but the 'K2s' differed by having English Electric controllers; otherwise the 300 vehicles were identical, making them the most numerous single type of London trolleybus. Three — Nos 1201, 1253 and 1348 — were preserved.
Geoffrey Morant/Photobus

A healthy crowd of passengers waits to board Green Line-liveried RF312 as it works Country Area route 447 in Reigate.
Geoffrey Morant/Photobus

Central Area-liveried RF405 is pictured heading towards Burnt Oak along route 251. Again it is noticeable how sparse the traffic is in this suburban street some 35 years ago. *Alastair Douglas/ Photobus*

The Underground

Although this book concentrates to a large extent upon the road vehicles of London Transport, it should not be forgotten that the decade was also a significant one for LT's other operation — the Underground. Growing up in south London, the author rarely had cause to use the Underground, but for countless others the Tube represented an essential means of travel.

Following the creation of the LPTB in 1933, there were great plans for the development and expansion of the Underground network. Announced in mid-1935, the New Works Programme envisaged, in co-operation with the main line railways, development of the Underground network to the north and east of London. In particular, the Central Line was to be extended eastwards to link up with the London & North Eastern Railway

lines towards Epping, which would be electrified, and the Northern Line was to be developed northwards and linked into the LNER lines serving Highgate, Alexandra Palace and Edgware. To the west of London, the Central Line was to be extended towards West Ruislip alongside the existing Great Western Railway route through Greenford.

Although the work was authorised and the funding in place, relatively little occurred before the outbreak of war caused, as elsewhere, a re-evaluation of priorities. Some of the work was completed — such as the link between the Bakerloo and Metropolitan lines north of Baker Street which allowed the former to take over operation of the line to Stanmore in November 1939 — whilst other work was in hand. Most notably, this was the laying of track for the Central Line extension to West Ruislip; however, this had not been electrified and the track was lifted for reuse elsewhere as a result of wartime exigencies. On the Northern Line, the two-mile extension from Highgate to East Finchley was opened on

▼

By the late 1950s, with the progress made on Metropolitan Line modernisation, time was running out for the locomotive-hauled services between Aylesbury and central London. Here ex-Metropolitan locomotive No 4 *Lord Byron* departs from Rickmansworth with a southbound service from Aylesbury in May 1959. The steam locomotive, which brought the train from Aylesbury, would have been removed at Rickmansworth. *G. M. Kichenside*

Following the construction of a number of prototype units in the mid-1930s, London Transport ordered in excess of 1,100 vehicles of 1938 stock. These coaches formed the basis of the rolling stock to be found on the Northern and Central lines through much of the decade featured in this book. The back of this official British Railways photograph states that a Bakerloo Line train is here approaching Hatch End alongside the Watford to Euston electric line on 25 August 1953.
British Railways

A District Line service for Mansion House is pictured at South Kensington station on 2 September 1958.
Dennis C. Ovenden

Pictured at Stratford, heading eastbound for Hainault on 6 October 1962, is this rake of 'silver' stock. In the late 1950s it was announced that London Transport was to order 76 rakes (formed of four plus three) of replacement rolling stock from Metro-Cammell for use on the Piccadilly Line. Delivery of the 1959 stock commenced at the end of that year. However, in order to assist in the modernisation of the Central Line, the last 57 rakes were to be transferred to the Central, with an additional 57 cars added to the order (the Central Line used eight-car rakes rather than seven). Additional rolling stock was ordered for the Central Line and those originally ordered for the Piccadilly — such as No 1277 seen leading the train here — were then transferred back to the Piccadilly Line, with the exception of the additional 57 coaches, which remained allocated to the Central.
Colin Boocock

3 July 1939, to be followed by a further extension, over electrified ex-LNER metals between East Finchley and High Barnet, on 14 April 1940. A further extension saw Northern Line services run from Finchley Central to Mill Hill East (on the line to Edgware) on 18 May 1941.

In the immediate postwar years, London Transport demonstrated considerable optimism that the New Works Programme would be reinstated after the cessation of hostilities. The familiar Beck maps of the era record the missing lines as either 'To be electrified' or 'Under construction'. In the event, the creation of the British Transport Commission forced the authorities into a re-evaluation of the various transport proposals and the bulk of postwar investment went into the main line railways rather than LT.

The Central Line extension beyond Liverpool Street, however, progressed. Services were extended to Stratford in December 1946 and thence to Leytonstone in May 1947. Part of this latter extension

was over ex-LNER metals transferred to London Transport. Later, in December 1947, LT electrified services were extended further eastwards, to Newbury Park and to Woodford. Newbury Park-Hainault saw electric services in May 1948 and the sections from Hainault to Woodford and from Woodford to Loughton followed in November the same year. The line from Loughton to Epping was electrified from September 1949; it was not, however, until 18 November 1957 that the final section of the ex-LNER line to Ongar was electrified. Elsewhere, the Central Line extension to West Ruislip, over lines relaid postwar, opened in two stages during 1947 and 1948. However, the further extension westwards to Denham was abandoned.

Also abandoned, and the largest casualty of the failure to complete the New Works Programme, were the Northern Line extensions north of Highgate and Edgware. In theory, LT had been scheduled to take over the ex-LNER line from Finsbury Park to

Alexandra Palace via Highgate. However, this scheme had not progressed before the war intervened and, when the British Transport Commission announced in late 1953 that the existing steam-operated service was to be withdrawn, the planned conversion did not proceed. Also abandoned, in 1950 and 1954 respectively, were the extensions of the Northern Line from Brockley Hill to Bushey and Edgware to Bushey. The link between Mill Hill East and Edgware was also dropped. Finally, abandoned in 1950 was the proposed southern extension of the Bakerloo Line from Elephant & Castle to Camberwell.

In 1956 the final piece of the planned New Works Programme — the modernisation of the outer sections of the Metropolitan Railway — was given the go-ahead. This work was to see the quadrupling of lines between Harrow-on-the-Hill and the point beyond Moor Park station where the Watford branch started, as well as electrification of the line from Rickmansworth to Amersham along

with the Chesham branch. In addition, the line was to be provided with new rolling stock. Electric services were introduced to the Chesham branch on 12 September 1960. Through Metropolitan services to Aylesbury — with a change of locomotive to BR steam at Rickmansworth — continued until 9 September 1961. From this date Aylesbury ceased to be a Metropolitan Line destination, being served instead by DMUs running to and from Marylebone station. The new rolling stock produced for the Metropolitan Line by Cravens of Sheffield was delivered in the early 1960s in the new standard unpainted aluminium.

London Transport in the 1950s — An Overview

The decade featured in this book was one of great change for London and for London Transport. The destruction wrought by the

◄ The most unusual variation on the RT theme were the 120 supplied by Cravens of Sheffield. As can be seen in this view of RT1413 working from Watford (WA) garage, it looked quite different from the standard version from every possible angle.

More typical are these two varieties seen parked outside Chelsham Garage. Pictured on the left is RT633, with the first type of roof box body, whilst on the right is RT2257 with a later standard body.

Although some tracks lasted for decades after the last trams had rolled over them, buried beneath the tarmac — one or two sections remain as I write — nearly all were taken up, a mammoth task that took many months. RT2527 heads along the wide Streatham High Road where the removal of the track is causing a lot less congestion than in the usually much narrower streets of south London. *V. C. Jones/Ian Allan Library*

RT43 of 1939, a New Cross bus, takes a breather on a summer day shortly after the last trams had departed the streets of Southeast London.

It has long been traditional for London double-deck buses to appear at the seaside, chiefly at summer weekends, sometimes on hire, sometimes organised by London Transport. I can recall a day out with my school to Battle and Hastings in a red RT from Croydon garage in 1950. Here RT2234 from Mortlake sits in the sun at Southsea in 1950, alongside a Duple-bodied Dennis Lancet belonging to one of the numerous Smiths that operated coach tours in the 1950s. *Dean Clark*

89

Reigate's RT1033, of November 1948 with an RT3/1-type body, sets off under the trolleybus wires along Station Road, West Croydon, on its long journey deep into Sussex where it will meet, *inter alia*, Southdown and Aldershot & District buses at its terminus in the Carfax at Horsham.

Goodwill visits abroad by London buses became a feature of the 1950s. Later, many London buses would find a home in far-flung parts of the world — earlier this year I watched several Routemasters through the spray of Niagara Falls as they conveyed sightseers along the Canadian bank. RTL1459 and RT 3710 head across a wet Putney Bridge prior to setting off for Zurich (where they carried 12,000 passengers), Germany, Denmark, Sweden and Belgium in the summer of 1953. *Ian Allan Library*

Luftwaffe during the war brought massive redevelopment to much of the Metropolis, whilst many of the traditional industries gradually declined. Changing social patterns — most notably the continuing expansion of the suburbs and the decline of the docklands — resulted in changing pressures upon London Transport.

At the start of the decade London Transport was faced by the need to complete the prewar process of tramway conversion — 'Goodbye, Old Tram', as Lord Latham so eloquently described it when the final London trams operated, a moment recorded for ever in that classic film of the end of London's trams *The Elephant will never Forget* — within a financial environment that made investment difficult.

For many tramway enthusiasts the end of London's tramways marked a defining moment in the gradual elimination of Britain's first-generation tramways. The interest aroused by the demise of the last trams was reflected in the amount of both colour film and transparencies taken at the time. July 1952 marked a watershed in many ways; one of the most important, and a reflection that postwar austerity was gradually coming to an end, was the availability of colour film. It was expensive and slow, but it did allow for scenes to be recorded for posterity that, had they happened even five years earlier, would have been less vividly portrayed.

The crowds that appeared for the final trams, and the emotional send-off that the last cars received, set a pattern for the last tram rites for the rest of the decade and, in London, was to be replicated towards the end of the decade by the gradual withdrawal of the trolleybuses.

Both trams and trolleybuses were considered, by their nature, to be potential contributors to road congestion. One of the most startling facets in examining many of the illustrations used in this book is the relatively low level of road transport. At the time, congestion was perceived as a problem and one that was getting considerably worse. Car ownership was undoubtedly on the increase and the amount of commercial goods carried by lorries was also increasing — the latter compounded by the fact that the railways ceased, during the decade, to be legally forced to be the common carrier.

The growth of road transport had one further major consequence apart from the increased congestion. Use of public transport was in decline. This meant that the anticipated traffic levels at the start of the decade, when public transport was still considered to be on the increase in passenger terms, proved to be illusory. London

Although the first London trolleybus routes to disappear, involving a physical diminution of the network, had been converted in the early 1950s, it was not until 1959 that the conversion of the world's then largest trolleybus system commenced. First to go, in March that year, were the routes based on the Bexleyheath and Carshalton depots. Short-wheelbase 'B1' No 92 of Carshalton, wearing its 23 years lightly, passes under the route 630 turning loop at West Croydon on 18 February 1959, two weeks before the end. This vehicle spent its entire life working from Sutton (later known as Carshalton) depot. The 'B1s' were fitted with special brakes in order to cope with the steep Anerley Hill at the Crystal Palace end of the route, a feature that was not considered necessary for the replacement diesel buses.

Because of the surplus of diesel-engined buses, the earliest replacement schemes used RTs and RTLs. The opportunity was taken to alter and extend former trolleybus routes, often bringing them right across the City of London and the West End. The 32 was a new route which followed that of the 661 between Leyton and Aldgate and then continued on to Victoria. RTL1294 heads down Bond Street having overtaken a United Dairies electric milk float.
W. H. R. Godwin

Transport reacted to this decline in two ways. Firstly, new vehicles were held in store rather than being put into traffic immediately, thereby resulting in a gradual diminution in the size of the fleet. Secondly, unremunerative routes were abandoned or reduced, a policy of retrenchment that was to lead to increasing problems with the labour force during the decade, resulting in periods of industrial action. The net result of these disputes was that passenger traffic further declined, resulting in yet more service reductions.

The decade was, however, not without benefits. The launch of the prototype Routemaster in 1954 and the first production models in 1959 helped to create a legend that, nearly a half-century later, still plies its trade on the capital's streets and is now universally recognised as a symbol of London. In the Routemaster, the designers produced the ultimate vehicle for handling the crowds in central London. On the Underground, despite the fact that certain elements of the New Works Programme were not completed, the expanded infrastructure and new rolling stock helped to ensure that the Tube was able to deal with the traffic growth of subsequent decades.

◄◄ As the trolleybus system shrank, newer vehicles were transferred to replace withdrawn older ones. This line-up at Paddington Green in June 1959 is headed by 'N1' No 1599, transferred from Bow. Next is one of the original 'C2' class, No 271, with only days to go, and bringing up the rear is 'N2' No 1635.

◄ The Routemaster has been a familiar sight on the streets of London for over 40 years. A remarkable sight at the Chiswick Works Golden Jubilee Gala on 2 July 1983 was this line-up of the first eight, RM1, in its present (modified) form, being nearest the camera.

T R U E   C O L O U R S

Ian Allan
PUBLISHING

Glory Days: Royal Blue
Colin Morris
ISBN: 0711027277 £15.99

Glory Days: BET Group
Gavin Booth
ISBN: 0711026092 £14.99

Glory Days: Green Line
Kevin McCormack
ISBN: 0711027307 £15.99

Glory Days: RT - The History of a Classic London Bus
Kevin McCormack
ISBN: 0711025819 £14.99

Glory Days: Tilling Group
Gavin Booth
ISBN: 0711025975 £14.99

Glory Days: Midland Red
Mike Greenwood
ISBN: 0711025894 £14.99

Glory Days: Scottish Bus Group
Gavin Booth
ISBN: 0711027102 £15.99